After All

Daryl Eigen

Copyright © 2015 Daryl Eigen

All rights reserved.

ISBN-10: 1514358301
ISBN-13: 978-1514358306

To Judy
Many blessings

Daryl Eigen

DEDICATION

JEEVANI

WHO SUPPORTED ME EVERY DAY

THE ALL IS EVERYTHING AND
EVERYTHING IS THE ALL.
---Daryl Eigen

Daryl Eigen

CONTENTS

ESSAYS

1. Down Sizing 3
2. Blackest Water 6
3. Donut Holes 8
4. Dignity for the Enemy 19
5. Dress Blues 23
6. Spirit is the Solution 25
7. Spirit's Abode 26
8. Freedom of Choice 28
9. The Meaning of Life 31
10. How Do You Feel? 33

EVERY DAY POEMS

11. The Road Ahead 35
12. Too Much Stuff 36
13. Carless and Carfree 38
14. Hiccups and Corners .. 40
15. Every Day Secrets 42
16. More or Less 44
17. Shades of Life............... 47
18. Puzzle Incomplete 49
19. Keep on Trucking 53
20. I Woke Up Dead 56

MIND POEMS

21. Shell Shocked Awakening 58

22. Sticky Pieces 62

23. All Pleasure Turns to Pain ..64

24. Stand Up 66

25. Panic Attack 67

26. Ocean of Tears 69

27. Time Passing 71

28. Feel Normal 74

29. Down Down Down 76

30. Limits 79

SPIRITUAL POEMS

31. Between My Thoughts ……... 81
32. Time Analysis ………………… 85
33. I Saw Him ……………………..88
34. By and By ……………………. 92
35. Pixelated Recycling ………. 94
36. Dark Matter …………………… 96
37. Too Many Lives ……………… 99
38. Writers Guild ………………… 101
39. Brick Wall ……………………… 103
40. That's All ……………………… 104

Note: The parenthetical numbers on some titles refer to the publication history of the essay or poem. See the publication list on page 105.

Daryl Eigen

ACKNOWLEDGMENTS

Thanks to the Albuquerque NM VA Hospital writing group for inspiration and patience.

After All

ESSAYS

1: Down-Sizing (1,2,4,10)

> You don't own your possessions, your possessions own you. ----- Satchidananda

We decided to retire, to down-size and to move. We went from 3800 square feet including storage to 935 square feet including storage. Those numbers implied a lot of stuff would have to go. Like bureaucracy stuff grows of its own accord. The more stuff you have the more stuff you need to take care of the stuff you have. Or you need some additional stuff to make the stuff you have complete or more usable. No matter how, stuff grows inexorably.

Stuff is at the heart of our materialistic culture. The number of people plus their stuff has grown to such a grand scale that it is affecting the health of our planet. Or so it is said. What is needed is a cultural shift to more mindfulness to change the dynamics of this global and individual problem of worldly excess. So I was helping the world by reducing our stuff. Somehow it did not feel so noble. I still have unopened boxes from 3 to 5 moves ago.

Getting rid of stuff by selling useful stuff on Craig's List and collectable stuff on Ebay was fun and lucrative. Even more successful and a kick to boot was renting a booth at the largest semiannual garage sale event in town. Less successful was selling larger items at auction. From then on it was a slog.

Down-sizing was the first step of repositioning us for the rest of our lives, but this put us right into our stuff! We were forced to deal with stuff at every level, inside and out. In dealing with the tangibles of our lives, I started dealing with our stuff on a spiritual level, as our stuff was very deeply intertwined with who we are.

I am seeking something greater than myself from within. But even though I am retired, it is still difficult to find time to pursue in detail my spiritual goals. I am too busy with my stuff.

As we shed things in a variety of ways, we obtained wisdom on how our attachments and desires made us addicted to stuff and how our stuff dictated portions of our lives. I have made much progress but I am not yet done. The stronger my spiritual practice the less attached I am to things and the more we can down-size.

Well we are moving again. We now have moved 9 times in 14 years, for work and other reasons, and we still have too much stuff. It is mostly the stuff we like or it would already be gone. It is the stuff that we have identified with and it is therefore a part of us. Some of it represents things we do not want to deal with and have been schlepping around for years. I will have to pack my things and face what they mean to me and decide if I can get rid of them. I can choose to make it a positive and meaningful experience or just pack everything without paying attention to what my stuff means or whether I will ever use it. I picked up an item from the floor where we were sorting our stuff for the move. I thought it best to ask myself some questions about its worth. Why did I buy this? Is it still usable? Will I need it? How probable is it that I will use it? Have I ever used it? Is it still in the original wrapper? Maybe it is collectable. While I am pondering its value my wife comes by and throws it in the donation pile with the admonition to leave it there and move on. No wonder I am writing this piece.

2: The Blackest Water (1,7)

It was February 17th, 1944, during WWII. Captain Yoshita walked the deck looking at the fleet ships resting in the calm waters while dawn was breaking over the Central Pacific. Seconds before the unseen torpedo exploded, the Captain saw the American planes. He realized that all was lost. The fleet was doomed. The Americans, with few casualties, finished the turkey shoot in 3 days.

The Ghost Fleet of the Pacific gradually turned into one of the premiere SCUBA dive spots in the world. I discovered first hand that wreck diving at Truk, now called Chuuk, is both thrilling and turn-your hair-white-overnight scary.

One hundred feet down with a new moon and cloudy skies, the water was blacker then anyone could imagine. I asked, "Who wants to go on a night dive?" Only one fellow diver volunteered. The rest sat silent until one of the women said, "Are you kidding? It is dark down there!" The volunteer and I smiled, suited up and entered the black water. Our headfirst descent into the eerie darkness went quickly. The sunken ship loomed large in the gloom of the dark water. Ahead of us was the spooky goal of our dive, an adjustable, surgical platform set in a wide-open space. It looked like the pilot seat of a very large alien ship. I began to imagine the screams, anguish, and suffering of those that manned this ship and died. My resolve to explore the ship started to wither.

    With bravado we propelled ourselves forward, deeper into the ship to get a closer look. It was then that I noticed several inches of silt covering everything. I tried to warn my dive buddy but I was too late. He hit the silt with a broad sweep of his fin. The silt swirled up like a wizard's smoke causing a blizzard. Our lights reflected off of the silt blinding us with scattered light and murkiness. We were lost in the wreck and had already been down too long. I felt panic sweep over my body with an irresistible urge to scramble to the surface, the bends and partners be damned. With all my will I resisted the fatal urge to flee. I slowed my breathing and tried to think.

    I grabbed my dive buddy, who was frozen with fear and turned us one hundred and eighty degrees. Swimming blind we moved through the ship and silt, groping along the way. We emerged into the uninterrupted, silent blackness of water. Rising with our bubbles, using the last of our air reserves, we ascended. Breaking through the surface I ripped off my mask to feel the freedom of being alive. The tropical air never smelled or tasted so good.

3: Donut Holes

Donut History, Architecture of the Universe, and the Collective Unconscious

(Warning: Satirical Essay)

The meeting was about a new phone. Sitting at a table with twelve other people, I watched the woman next to me push the box of donut holes in my direction, just like the three times before. I observed the tradeoff of desire, politeness, and dedication to diet that resulted as the donut holes were passed. It was a struggle for almost everyone at the table except for the ambitious and gluttonous who abstained and binged respectively. I was on the cusp of both and thus neutralized into following the donut holes as they went round, round, and round like a bouncing ball in a sing-a-long-cartoon. The monotonous drone of my boss's voice lulled me into a hypnogogic epic dream about the poly-technical evolution of the cosmic doughnut theory.

One morning after coffee and sweet fried dough, in the mid 19th century, Captain Hansen Gregory had a Freudian epiphany while precariously turning his schooner into the wind. Simultaneously holding his holeless fried dough and a cup of rum-spiked coffee, he spun the pilot wheel with one hand to execute the maneuver. Suddenly the main sail ripped straight up the middle making a screeching sound. In an attempt to recover, he smashed his fried dough onto one of the wheel spokes, creating a hole in the center of the fried sweetness. His newly discovered 'knot-of-dough' with a hole was crispy outside with firm cake inside. Thus the donut was born. Captain Gregory was not the Earl of Sandwich but darn close.

Fast forward one hundred years; In the twentieth century the donut was commercialized by a company named Dunking Doughnuts. Marketing was done through signage, newspaper ads and comic book back pages. Super heroes were used in the comic book ads. Each superhero required special donut contract riders whenever an ad appeared. The Green Lantern wanted green donuts, the Hulk wanted huge green donuts, and Flash wanted any donuts fast. And there was social media: WOM, Word-of-Mouth, was the telephone party line where many homes shared a single phone line and took turns using it. Phyllis, the switchboard operator chatted with all the neighbors and could listen in on any call she wanted. She was the social network. Soon everyone knew of the commercial donut that was made for dunking. To be able to buy one with a cup of coffee at a store that only sold donuts and coffee was a revolutionary idea that required a shift in consumer consciousness. Dunking Doughnuts spawned this new thinking as they bravely grew stores from coast to coast as if that was their manifest destiny. In the Great West people went from town to town on the train looking for Dunking Doughnuts.

The Chinese heard about the American donut frenzy from their grandparents who had laid train track across the US. The Chinese immediately said they invented the donut centuries ago. No surprise there. The Chinese donut was called youtiao for 'dough stick'. When it was pointed out that it was a fried stick of dough and not a donut, they said all they had to do was to connect the ends and, voila, a donut. 'Voila' is French and not Chinese, a stick is not a donut, and a one is not a zero. "Or are they two sides of the same donut? Hmmm", as Mike Myers might say.

The Arabs said they invented the Zero but it first came from the Babylonians, then the Mayans and finally the East Indians where it was invented again. Although it was nothing, it resembled the hole in the donut close enough to gain respect. It was amazing how fast nothing made it around the globe, notwithstanding that there was nothing the people of the time did not like. No matter what they say, the Chinese were not involved.

As WWII wound down, the German and French philosophers struggled with the new object and argued back and forth about donut and nothingness, and its ontology. How did the donut come into existence? How is it that something, the donut, came from nothing, the donut hole, or more formally the hole in the donut?

In the last few days of the war, shortly before he committed suicide, Hitler turned over the 3rd Reich to Grand Admiral Donitz, pronounced Donuts if spoken quickly. His rein as president lasted 20 days. He no doubt spent his days eating Berliners, a type of donut with no central hole, in a bunker somewhere near the Netherlands' border. Years later President Kennedy would say in a speech in West Berlin the famous line "Ich bin ein Berliner" which means, in the colloquialism of the time and place "I am a donut." The point was to show unity of the free world with the people of West Berlin. That would be "Ich bin Berliner". "I am from Berlin". No one cared.

In the mid 1900s the donut came in three flavors: plain, plain, and plain like the three colors of the telephone, black, black and black. In the late 1960s color options came for both the phone and the donut. The age of the donut had begun. The donut circled the globe bringing the power of the donut wherever it went. Wherever it traveled, there it was. A simple turn of the donut could cause a wedding banquet in New Deli, a variation of the butterfly effect.

The new age attracted philosophers, mathematicians, physicists, psychologists, and engineers who thought deeply about the donut. A Zen Master realized that the donut bounded the hole in an unending circle that represented the emptiness of being. Another Zen Master from a different province sat in meditation in front of a whitewashed board without food, water or facilities. He held his ink filled calligraphic brush ready for three days. Suddenly, in a single stroke of genius, he stood and inked a rough donut on his board to symbolize the nature of life or Buddha nature. He grunted "enzo", which means donut-like in Japanese.

An Indian sadhu decided that his austerity was to eat only the holes in donuts. His Guru said in a heavy East Indian accent, "Don't be silly, that is nothing to fool with. Go to your cave and live on whatever the universe offers. Before you eat, say a prayer so it is holy. Then you can eat holy things, like the donut."

All the while mathematicians concentrated on the shape of the donut. To make it more general, they called it a torus, math-speak for donut and, for that matter, the bagel; Not to offend the bagel but that is another story riddled with guilt fillings. As they studied the torus they came to realize that it was an object with one hole. Topology, the study of holes, says an object with one hole can be morphed or stretched into any object with one hole. The mathematicians went a step further and looked at the hole of nothingness in the donut and figured out how to derive the infinity of numbers from nothing, like a magicians hat. Multiple infinities followed quite unexpectedly. The cardinal infinities are labeled with the first letter of the Hebrew alphabet, Aleph, and a subscript starting with naught. It goes on and on and on. New numbers were discovered including the surreal numbers that may be the basis for this surreal dream.

The physicists were not to be ignored. They realized that the universe is a multiverse that resolves issues in quantum theory. A different universe may be created with every particle interaction. This is a very large finite number. There may be an infinite number of universes, because there is enough room in the infinities of numbers to allow universes to be created to house our dreams, imagination, literature, heavens and hells. If all these universes were removed from the meta-verse there would still be room for an infinity of possible worlds. If this were true than Carl Jung would be vindicated because there would be universes in which synchronicity was a physical law.

Physicists applied theory to the cosmos and found out there are holes in space that are so big and have so much gravity that they suck in all matter in their vicinity, both light and dark, ending in a singularity which is another way of saying infinity. These celestial holes are called black holes by scientists who drank their coffee black, of course. It only takes two dimensions to describe a black hole, but this only creates more issues. The topology of the universe is very complex because it has so many holes. Black holes are invisible because no light can escape. All matter that falls into a black hole gets ripped apart and pulverized into nothingness. Watching a black hole eat its neighbors reminds one that one must be careful whom one sits next to at the counter of a local Dunking Doughnuts shop.

A black hole has an event horizon or point of no return beyond which you, a sun, a galaxy or a donut cannot be observed. An event horizon is like a donut that has been dunked too long. There is a point at which the effects of dunking are irreversible.

Can you see the donut dunking droppings at the bottom of the cup? We may be living in two dimensions like the black hole and a third dimension that is a holographic projection. Our perception of our three dimensional world may be equal to a holographic multi-holed donut. The mathematicians gave the donut a more definitive name, torus or the toroid ring polyhedral, made up of multiple annuluses.

We do not necessarily know the difference between a holographic projection and reality. All of our sensory input is broken down into electrochemical signals. So we are not experiencing reality directly. On the other hand, physical reality may not be that substantial. The smallest particles that make up our world seem to have an information quality like a bit, one or zero. The world is an illusion that the ancient masters always said it was. Maybe we are in a giant simulation run by a mad software engineer nerd who herself is in a universe simulation.

The collective unconscious is very deep and dark like space. Psychologists who explored the depths of mind never go too deep without a flashlight, a cordless phone and a donut. Donuts help answer the question of how the deep unconsciousness of one person can be connected to everyone else. This conjecture requires that the outside have continuity with the inside, thus the donut. The landscape of the field of consciousness, is curved not unlike the curvature of space as discovered by Einstein in his general theory of relativity. Like the universe, the topology of the collective unconscious may have multiple holes, one or more per person depending on the diagnosis.

At the exact moment I am dreaming that I am writing about synchronicity, I dreamt that my donut fell to the floor seemingly without any help other than from gravity and synchronicity. Or is this an audible omen to tell me to wake up? But on I dream, clearly in need of therapy or a donut.

The sense of self must be the cause of these holes in the collective unconscious, I pondered. The holes in the fabric of our being are burnt by the ego and can only be filled with the light of Spirit. Every pleasure ends in pain, so say the Yoga Sutras. As tasty as a donut is, eventually it will be eaten causing the pain of loss and separation, aka donut withdrawal. Once awareness dawns the myriad of holes will most likely disappear and be seen as reflections of one hole, the Maha hole.

The psychologists, physicists and philosophers continued to argue about donut and nothingness until the cows came home to provide cream for their coffee. Meanwhile the donut wars began. The donut was already an archetype on its way to becoming an icon. The marketers thought of new ways the donut could be made with chocolate, sprinkles, blueberries, toppings, and icings. The lead engineer, filled with ire and sugared donuts, interacted with a deficit of interpersonal skills with testing landing him somewhere on the autism spectrum. He screamed "You are ruining the dunking properties of the donut. You are forcing the dunking index below pi." The marketers thought he meant pie (P I E), an old foe of the donut. The cry of the engineer was ignored. Marketing did not care because the Family Feud survey said that the only dunking going on was by the Jay Leno age groups and they were:

1. Alive when there were letters in their phone number.

2. Not allowed to eat fried dough.

3. Unable to dunk a basket much less their donut.

4. Policemen who would rather not ruin a perfectly good donut by dunking it.

Of the total market only 20% dank, past tense of dunk, and the dunkers were projected to dwindle not grow. The growth market was the dunk-less youth. Thus the enigma of Leno's departure from TV was solved.

With the dwindling of dunking, Dunking Doughnuts almost sustained global extinction. The Crispy Cream donut went viral. The company used a new method to make the donut less caloric and lighter. People went crazy for this fluffy stuff. Some said it was the holiest of donuts and some said it was evil. It was just like when people went crazy for the cordless telephone.

The new donut won the wars for a while. Then one day an entrepreneur came up with the idea of selling the actual holes of the donut, the centers of nothingness. Engineers were happy because the diameter for dunking was right; Customers might burn their fingers, but the engineers seemed unconcerned. The lawyers were happy because someone was going to get burned and subsequently sue. The marketers were happy because the hole was a smaller bite option that weight watchers could love. The environmentalists were happy because there was less waste. The existential philosophers were happy because they found the missing piece of nothing that was something thus there was nothing that wasn't something. Crispy Cream and Dunking Doughnuts became the giants of the donut industrial complex and settled into a comfortable cease-fire that evolved into a duopoly of the industry.

Product wars follow the evolutionary law of 'survival of the fittest' but in a shorter time frame. In response to the pressures of survival and extinction, new evolutionary product species emerged from the micro donut makers. Clearly there was only time for intelligent design. From the Donut Wars, circa 1980, some small donut makers had the maneuverability to make custom donuts, healthy donuts, exotic spiced donuts, gluten-free donuts, and hypoallergenic donuts. Their creativity went wild and so did sales, marking a spectacular explosion of donut species in the history of donut evolution. The dinosaur donut makers spent their time in meeting rooms, passing and eating donut holes while trying to figure out how to fight back. But most of the time they talked about the donuts their mothers used to make. Donut war casualties mounted even higher when donut companies were outflanked in the Cup Cake Wars that followed. No telling where donut interspecies breeding would lead. Dunking Doughnuts, in self defense, started selling sandwiches.

People had a hole in their donuts that science could not fill. It became clear that the donut was the way people could seek Spirit like the Zen masters and gurus before them. The goal of which was the understanding of the ultimate meaning of life. We are not separate from the donut, we are the donut, and there is only the donut. Some people filled the hole with more donuts.

In the 1990's neural scientists then discovered how a Zen Master could sit in meditation and surf the donut universe. By navigating the outside donut and traveling inward on the topological surface of the universal donut hole, he could grasp the whole. An aha moment ensued. He had navigated a two dimensional universe and broken through the projection of a third dimension. With a single puncture the donut turned inside out. He created a new Zen koan to provide a way to follow his path to enlightenment. What is the sound of an unstruck donut hole?

As people became heavier due to eating too many donuts, alternative medicine was consulted. Ancient medicine (ayurveda and Chinese acupuncture) is holistic and sees the body as a donut. The two primary openings are really only one hole that was stretched into a tube from one end to the other surrounded by donut like flesh and limbs. Their advice was to stop eating so much, especially fried food with wheat, like donuts, which would eliminate the donut around one's middle. No one listened.

Suddenly a phone rang disturbing my reverie and causing my chin to slip off my supporting hand. With a jerk I was forced back into reality. I looked up and saw the box of donut holes making its way around the table again, changing lives, changing waistlines, and changing the way we view the world. When the box arrived at my position I opened it. It was empty.

4: Dignity for the Enemy:

A Human Journey

Everyone deserves to experience basic human dignity, even one's enemies. Enemies are created through hatred and enmity and can be transformed to friendship and amity.

What is it about humankind that warrants so much strife in the world? Conflict occurs at every level of the world order, in every aspect of life, and in every corner of the mind. Wars proliferate between countries over territory, power and religious beliefs. War has come home and is expressed in schools, on army bases, and in mall shootings. We are inured to gang-related neighborhood drive-byes, workers going 'postal', and domestic disturbances. Thus the enemy is everywhere and if we don't want to harm ourselves through the psychological destruction that goes along with hate, we must figure out how to transform our mindset from a position of enmity to one of amity.

Terrorism and conflict has a disproportionate effect on our psyches relative to the actual number of people harmed. By way of comparison, genocide is disproportionate in a different manner. Last century alone marked the eradication of over 150 million people. In an effort to feel safer, we have militarized our police forces as evident in the number of recent police shootings of unarmed citizens. This is proof enough that we are in a state of strife and the creation of more enemies is the result.

War, struggle, and conflict express themselves in the world only if there is conflict in people's minds. Francis Meeham said, "There is only war between us because (we) are at war with (ourselves)". It is hard to fathom our responsibility for the conflict in the world. This strife may be ameliorated with a greater understanding of our contribution to this reverberating global, local, and individual violence. If war is a function of internal turmoil, then life's vicissitudes and our reactions to them are also dictated by one's state of mind. Applying dignity to the enemy is an antidote to the insipid, extensive and horrific violence that exists internally and externally.

> If there is to be peace in the world
> There must be peace in the nations
> If there is to be peace in the nations
> There must be peace in the cities
> If there is to be peace in the cities
> There must be peace between neighbors
> If there is to be peace between neighbors
> There must be peace in the home
> If there is peace in the home
> There must be peace in the heart
> ---Lao Tze (Good Reads Quotes)

My father always said I was fighting my self. Since I ended up on the frontlines of Vietnam a few years later, I now see that he had a point. Having experienced war firsthand in Vietnam as a young Marine, I wondered then and now at the utility of what we were doing. I fought against enemy forces in Con Thien and in the vicinity of the DMZ (Demilitarized Zone). I saw the true face of war. The sacrifices of many of my brothers-in-arms had no enduring value other than their shinning examples of courage and self-sacrifice. Not many people experience close quarters combat. It is rare for even those in uniform. Standing on the battlefield with the enemy approaching and good men dying with dignity, I can say the experience of war is truly of the world gone mad.

I have experienced war and met the enemy on the battlefield. And I have made enemies in my life, some from strength and some from weakness. I now do what I can to ameliorate the residual enemies that haunt the battlefield in my mind. I apply dignity to my enemies by considering them worthy and applying compassion. I forgive them and do not hate them or myself. When I got home I took my weapons to the river that ran through the center of town. On a bridge I looked down at the smooth and slow running water and tossed my weapons into the murk. The concentric ripples radiated outward and I prayed for peace in my lifetime.

The hope is that people become calmer and thus less prone to violence and by extension less likely to go to war or be agitated in mind or disruptive in life. The hope is for serenity and peace. Individuals can mark their progress by the lack of strife in their relationships, life and mind. Those caught in the web of war can achieve a sense of honor, solidarity and equanimity in the face of the cruelest of circumstances in an unjust war, if the mind is focused on applying dignity to the enemy externally and internally.

5: Dress Blues (1,7)

As soon as I turned 18, I joined the United States Marine Corps. Its image and strength were embodied in the Marine Corps dress blues that were worn on formal occasions, honor guard for the dead and on recruiting posters. The dress blues project the quiet, steely-eyed courage that protected our nation since 1776 not to mention the way it attracted the opposite sex. Or so the recruiter said. The tall stiff collar protected the throat from sword swipes and historically made of leather is the reason Marines are called leather-necks. I was also told that when I became an NCO (Noncommissioned Officer), I would rate an NCO sword to go with the dress blues and, of course, the medals. I thought "How cool is that?" But as it turns out I never wore and never owned dress blues or a sword even though I rated them.

In Boot Camp I was given basic issue with no regard to size or fit. I just had gear thrown at me as I was pushed and yelled through the supply hut. After Boot Camp I was officially a Marine, my service uniforms were issued and tailored. I also had green utilities for everyday duty that I starched for that crisp look. My chest anticipated medals and ribbons but remained empty for now. Dress blues would have to wait, as they would not be needed where I was going.

In the flick of an eye I was in the jungles of Vietnam. Without a shower or clothing change for months at a time my uniform was in tatters like the

American Flag over Ft. Sumpter. The jungle slowly rotted my uniform, skin and spirit. I earned some medals and ribbons but lost interest in military life as death persevered. The uniform of the day for some Marines was a grey body bag. Since I carried a radio it was my somber duty to call in a chopper to collect the deceased and wounded. In the incessant monsoon rain and mud I would pop a smoke grenade to mark the LZ. The smoke blew around in crazy patterns forced by the whirling blades of a chopper. The grey body bags, an ignominious uniform that no one willingly wore, were quickly loaded on the chopper as soon as it landed.

When I returned back to the US from my tour in Vietnam my interests waned. I had wanted to be an honor guard in dress blues to honor the dead and our flag. But medals or not I felt stripped of worthiness by the great meat grinder that was Vietnam. I just wanted to cry for the lost lives of my fellow Marines. I hoped the fallen would be buried in dress blues to signify the honor and sacrifice they made. Now I am older and over my fantasy of war and of uniforms except for the one thing I remember fondly. A good uniform acted like an aphrodisiac. Maybe that was the main reason I chose the Corps. But now I probably would have trouble buttoning my jacket.

6: Spirit is the Solution (1, 3)

Spirit is that which is unseen and intangible, as opposed to the physical and mundane. Spirit is ineffable, supernal and infinite. Spirit has to do with deep, often religious, feelings, including a person's sense of peace, purpose, connection to others, and beliefs about the meaning of life and a feeling of being in the flow.

Spirit demands a high degree of connectedness and presence. Spirit can be reached and personally experienced through the practice of Yoga and Buddhism to name just two.

Spirit is the only aspect of creation that can repair the tear of existential despair in the warp and woof of our being. Our maniacal relationship with stuff can be gently addressed by working with spiritual techniques that bring one into the presence of spirit. Un-needed stuff will be shed and slip away! In a life of experience how does one find out how he or she feels and believes? Too often the judgment of others and cultural norms dictates what a person believes. On the other hand, the life of spirit can only be experienced internally to oneself. No statistics apply because it is a sample size of one: you. No one or no thing can tell you what your internal experience is. Your internal experience is only yours. People can tell you their internal experience that may or may not match your experience. The Buddha implores us to not take anything at face value but rather to explore what is true for each of us.

7: Spirit's Abode (1,7)

We are all made of the same stuff. It is the stuff of the universe large and small. Stuff makes up the physical world with fields that are infinite. We, and everything we experience, are part of the field. There is only the field. We are infinite. Stuff is made up of smaller stuff like atoms. And atoms are made up of even smaller stuff like protons and smaller than small stuff called quarks and leptons among other things. These particles can also be waves when unobserved. Quarks can be strange, charm, up, down, top and bottom but these are just names. There may be even smaller realms where stuff is stranger still. These small pieces of stuff are perhaps so small that they may never be directly observed. The smallest stuff in the world may not be a particle or wave in nature at all but be more like bits of information: 1s and 0s. A bit is ethereal and has no substance. It is not too much of a stretch to imagine that at these very small scales spirit abides. So when we look at and feel our surroundings, know that there is depth to our vision and that the sense of solidity is an illusion of one force field touching another because stuff is mostly space, nothingness or zero. An information bit is either zero or one. If matter is a one then space maybe a zero. Energy is the cosmic computation filled with movement of 1s and 0s. Spirit is infinite and not computable. Spirit is not zero nor one as it is indivisible while nature is not. Spirit in nature is a reflection of the Spirit alone and as such has its own place in the fabric of the universe.

On a much larger scale, ancient, huge stars

implode into black holes creating heavier elements in the process. Most of these elements have been around for a very long time. We are not separate from our surroundings. I mean this in the strongest possible way. We exchange atoms with our fellow humans and other creatures on this planet by breathing and eating or just by the fuzzy atomic edge of the semi-boundary between who we are or what we think we are and everything else. We may be built of atoms that were incorporated into Benjamin Franklin's rotund frame or Buddha's belly. From the largest scale to the smallest scale we are an animated pattern within an animated pattern. The patterns are also the stuff dreams are made of as life is just a dream. There is no "I" within this torrential pattern of ones and zeros. If we let spirit and the universe flow through us, we will obtain what we need. And we will feel calm and aligned with what is. The universe has an order to it; otherwise all would be in chaos. If you trust the universe you can create peace by letting go of things, feelings, thoughts, and programmed actions. If spirit is in the smallest realms of reality then it is everywhere and in everything.

8. Freedom of Choice

We experience making choices in a way that has us believing we are the chooser. And we therefore think we are in control of the consequences. This is a misrepresentation that our sense of self (ego) perpetrates. The ego claims credit and responsibility for choices and consequences.

The sense of self (ego) is the keeper and creator of the story line of our lives but is not the chooser. It is the recorder. Our understanding and image of ourselves consciously making a choice is a self-serving fantasy.

Experiments reveal that our perception of making a choice comes some time after the actual choice has been made. Our image and understanding of the world around us is thus a post hoc construction of events. If awareness of a choice is after the fact then how can we make a choice at all much less a good one?

Choices in the now create consequences in the future. So if we want a better future that is more real and more in our control we have to concentrate internally and become consciously aware of the ego illusion. Then we will have a view to the mechanisms of choice and some control over our lives.

One can judge the goodness of choice by its consequences. Unfortunately it is impossible to know the full impact of any decision we make. With every choice a network of predicted and unknown consequences ripple forward in time. The law of unintended consequences comes into play. Future events may happen from choices we make that are counter productive to the intentions of our original choice.

Choice is accessible internally where and when consciousness of our state of mind becomes clearer and calmer. Reactivity to any situation obviates our ability to choose. In the unconscious state of being distracted, disorganized, emotional, or reactive one is confused about what choice to make or even sometimes that there is a choice.

Our internal experience and reduction of ego can aid us in making the best choices. We assume and often demand to choose our path in life but then falsely claim it is destiny or fate. Freedom of choice and destiny are opposites and cannot coexist moment to moment just like dark of night cannot exist in the light of day.

Our choices precipitate consequences. Consequences are a response from the universe. We unconsciously react to the universe's response and then the universe responds ad infinitum. This tumble through time is our destiny and not our choice. Unfortunately without awareness and control one's destiny may entail a very bad trajectory.

Consciousness, awareness and focus without the sense of self or ego are the groundwork for making good choices.

We have to be committed to making our own choices. There needs to be enough focus to have access to the decision process. We must make the best choice we can, knowing that the future consequences may not always bounce the way we foresee. Freedom of choice requires that we be conscious that there are choices to be made.

To choose wisely we are required to observe our thoughts and control them; thus neutralizing the ego inspired view of our selves. In this way we can make good choices and increase the likelihood of manifesting a desirable outcome.

Even if awareness and control are firmly established our influence and choice making are only relevant for a limited time. The world is impermanent and everything changes including the opportunities for choice making.

9: The Meaning of Life

Standing on the battlefield with the enemy approaching and good men dying with dignity, the "fog of war" (MacNamera) obscured any clarity of meaning of what Vietnam (or war) was all about. Like Iraq, Vietnam was (in Rumsfeld's famous obfuscation) an 'un-known un-known'. Later with an amplified awareness and presence developed in war to stay alive, life became more vivid. The 'Band of brothers' (Shakespeare) only fought for the survival of each other. While solidarity on the battlefield was a transcendent experience it was only the beginning. I was guided to read the ancient masters to clarify an understanding of what life was all about.

Patanjali's Yoga Sutras is an ancient sacred text. Patanjali, offers that the meaning of life has two purposes (PII.21). One is liberation and the other is to experience the joy of life. Patanjali makes no judgments or efforts to proselytize about which path should be taken. The tools are provided in the Sutras to live better in either case. Meditation and spiritual practice will benefit all even if one just wants to live for experience. Spiritual practice calms the mind and relieves suffering or at least modifies our attitude toward it. Viktor Frankl gets at the core. Frankl talks about the last human freedom in his "Man's Search for Meaning":

"Every thing can be taken from man but one thing: the last human freedom -- - to choose one's attitude in any given circumstances, to choose one's own way.

Patanjali offers us a choice and the opportunity to be of service to all. The world can change with every choice we make from moment to moment. We can make the choice consciously or unconsciously. We cannot know the future but we can affect it. Thus it is suggested that we make considered choices. It will be more likely that the world will change in a positive way with consciously positive choices. Making spiritual choices and doing regular spiritual practice will help guarantee a better life, so say the ancient enlightened ones. Choosing to not make war is a better choice unless justice need prevail. War is a wound that needs to be healed or prevented on both sides, win or loose. All need realize that hurting another is hurting one's self. It is our choice.

10: How Do You Feel?

The question of the decade is "How do you feel? " It is not just something I noticed. The question used to be more behavioral.

How are you doing? This is often spoken in passing and not meant. It is an idiomatic expression. When you say it as a throw away greeting surprisingly some will tell you how terrible or good their life is.

What do you do? This is often the second question asked. I am not my job. Anyway I am retired. Next comes what are you thinking? In fact I am not thinking at all but just standing here feeling the wind in my hair. The telling phrase is, what were you thinking? I obviously did something wrong.

Now the first question is, How did you feel when anything changes or occurs. For example, how did it feel going over the waterfall in a little boat? We want to share in the experience without the risk.

How do you feel?

EVERY DAY POEMS

11: THE ROAD AHEAD (1,3)

Thinking about the road ahead

some years to be done and dead.

I wanted to get ahead

instead I went back to bed.

Arising again to be fed.

Butter both sides the morning bread.

 How about some jam I said.

 Live, pray, and love instead.

 Look back blessings count.

 Let life's ledger take account.

 Your life amounts

 to all the battles

 and lesser routes.

12: TOO MUCH STUFF

There is too much stuff

and too many things.

It is never enough

to live like kings.

Old cars in the back do rust.

Items unused collect dust.

Our desires are a must

so we buy until we bust.

Wheels of industry whirr

making things we never use.

In larger and larger numbers

It is all good, too good

the future blind with things.

Unknown where we stood

we continue to collect.

We shop, shop, shop

After All

making it harder not to stop.

Slave to the coming bill.

Buy, buy, buy we will.

Never ever to be still.

We live in a world of stuff.

Not important, just fluff.

Let's go back to the store;

who cares there's always more.

13: CARLESS CARFREE

I love cars but

I sold my car.

I SOLD MY CAR!

My only car,

to save the planet;

to save myself;

to save money.

I am car free.

No need to worry

about a ding

or anything.

Nothing to wash,

nothing to crush

I use car2go and Zip

but Uber is mighty hip.

Busses and taxis still work.

After All

An old school quirk.

As do street cars and rail

or walking on the trail.

A car can be rented

without being dented.

Biking is a way to go

It helps to show

that we are serious

to get where we are going

in full awareness and knowing

the ins and outs of our mission

to lower our carbon emissions.

14: HICCUPS AND CORNERS

Life is a line without dimension.

Driven by our imagined past and

future expectations.

God give us a sign.

Always distracted, missing cues

on we barrel paying no heed

gaining speed our pain protracted.

On the tracks unable to divert

unknown awaits hidden from view.

In slow motion our line cracks.

The track looks straight:

a ruse--- a corner appears

to nowhere.

A loose screech

After All

sounds a life about to crumble.

Not so bad, we cry.

All that gnashing and drama.

Your OK we say.

Too many corners, too many surprises.

From the future not unexpected.

Just a hiccup, we say

Wishing straight lines

the rest of the way.

Daryl Eigen

15: EVERYDAY SECRETS

Every day I think of that time

long ago when I was crazy.

I have a secret, I will never tell.

I hurt some people, hope they are well

Wait for the knock perhaps there are more.

I have secrets boiling over.

Did you think there was only one?

How many people are looking?

 I am not hiding alone.

No amends can be made

No matter if they hound.

But they are not looking

or I would be found.

Daryl Eigen

Looking for them

yields nothing.

They must be gone

Not a visit not a clue.

Same goes for me.

Let sleeping dogs lie.

I don't want to see

what I may have done to thee.

16: MORE OR LESS

What was the core?

What did she want?

She wanted less

he wanted more.

She could see the future;

one day it was true.

On Wednesday she left

he buried in brew.

Life moved along

healing no wounds.

She far too cruel

he sang no song.

No one's fault.

Lies were spun.

Daryl Eigen

None were caught

by heart's alum.

Life came and went

without event.

Darkness in the corner

sadness did not prevent.

Dull grey overcame

all that was worthy.

Haunting drops of rain

dampened all reverie.

She hardly missed him.

He pined for the loss.

She laughed over sparkle.

He over albatross.

    One tear it wrought.

After All

One day to finish

with more not less.

17: SHADES OF LIFE

Lives exist on belief

that life is all too brief

to be filled with grief.

In an arch of arbor

 scattered papers liter the ground.

Leaving a trail yet to be found.

Swirling dirt devils

promise change.

May the wind blow

colors into every

aspect of cold.

Hints of winter rearrange

the open range for miles.

After All

The burning of the piles

smoke and clear misdeeds

and more regrets.

Lives are written on scraps of paper.

The good ones live on

to blow in the wind.

Others turn black

and edges glow red when burning.

18: PUZZLE INCOMPLETE

An old puzzle just found

Too long has been around.

Let's put it together

and see if it's sound.

Understand not

just filling spaces,

paper faces and

worn places.

Complexity

hides the crime.

Forever broken

beyond time.

A bird's shadow

After All

eclipses the moon

fluttering wings

a somber tune.

Nothing transcends

pictures forgotten

just rows and ends.

Walking circles

Struggle to fit.

Searching for something

that will click.

.

Pray mystery

no pattern breaks.

Try another edge

a key that creates.

Random pieces

scattered in rows.

Daryl Eigen

With each piece

the puzzle grows

Finally it shows

a murder of crows

On a wintery tree

oddly looking at me.

The haunting picture

allures completion.

A piece still missing

upon reflection.

Look on the floor

around the table

perhaps your pocket

finish one more.

But notice the birds

flying at the window

After All

and knocking at the door.

The offending piece is dancing

on the floor forever more.

Daryl Eigen

19: KEEP ON TRUCKING

I waited at the corner

with asphalt at my back.

Trying to rise but felt the lack

of strength I must garner.

Legs are like lead

Unable to lead

My left eye blinking

My right brain thinking.

Trying to get home

No one answers the phone

Help is needed still.

I am really undeniably ill.

I don't remember what hit me

After All

It hardly was a tree

No one was left to see

appalling though my condition be.

Someone gave me a dollar

I had more in my pocket

Never mind whether alive or not

Need one good Samaritan to holler

911! Pain fierce as the sun.

No one noticed my bleeding brain

A random slip, how mundane

Please call an ambulance

While I wait for the truck

Blindly cursing my luck.

Sprawled In the lane I began to swear

I needed an ER not a buck

On Earth just a guest

Daryl Eigen

waiting with interest

death on the crest.

After All

20: I WOKE UP DEAD

I woke up dead

a round in my head.

Is it something I said?

Try heaven instead.

Time slowed down

doors all closed.

Tibetan drums

sound faintly.

Or did I drown?

I was already gone

crossed over to the light.

In far away song

celestial rainbows did sight.

Wondering if I did enough right.

The doctor yelled:

"1,2,3 clear". Buwapp "1,2,3 clear".

Daryl Eigen

Muffled words bantered here.

Something about organ donors.

WHAT?

I bolted straight up

Beep…, beep…, beep.

Like a dead man with rigor

my heart beat…beat…beat

as if I had vigor.

Everyone jumped back

not ready for me to stay.

Not to die that day.

But not for lack

of struggle with the black.

Eyes partially open

I needed to rest.

Nearing the end of my quest

To battle windmills and less.

After All

MIND POEMS

Daryl Eigen

21: Shell Shocked Awakening (8)

Not knowing who he was;

remembering that he was.

Not knowing where or

why or when it was

or how he got there.

Just remembering

he was someone.

Not able to speak.

with nothing to say.

He remembered.

People came and went,

asking questions.

After All

answered by silence.

Filled with dread that turned to love,

He wandered from his fighting hole.

On the way to grace,

with mouth full of dirt,

he became elevated and revealed

on the bloody field.

A spark from the bonfires

of artillery boxes

set him off.

Like the flares lighting the muddy land

a humble agent, able to walk the earth.

Not a fallen agent,

but a silent invisible winged force.

People are looking for him.

Crazy they say,

Daryl Eigen

maybe in a good way, maybe not.

What should one do when cast to earth?

Find a comfortable place to sit.

Look down and see

through the body of life

spheres, molecules,

particles , subtle energies,

and animated processes inside and out.

Be a transparent part of everything.

Made of the same stuff

as the patch of grass upon which he sits.

The breaking fiery dawn brings happiness.

After so many days just rest.

If only he could talk,

he could tell us about the that, that is all.

22: Sticky Pieces

We can always tell

what's gone awry.

We feel it when we cry

or try to fill it with a lie.

No one's complete.

It's why we yell at the start.

And why the hole in our heart.

We can tell who we are

 by what we are not.

Defined by what we never had.

Just what we needed no matter how sad.

Were we really so very bad?

It's not the material things.

It's all the same for paupers or kings

We don't feel complete

After All

 if it is money we seek.

Of this secret we never speak.

 about wisdom.

We just have

sticky pieces that don't belong

making nights very long.

How can we forgive a foe

If tomorrow we can't let go.

Deep inside where we cannot peek

hidden regrets, slights, errors and repeats

Lost in muck; forever stuck.

What awaits us is not too late.

Grateful our burden is not too great.

23: All Pleasure Turns to Pain (6)

Pleasures are many.

Some are uncanny.

But none last a life-time

or even a day.

With fun to be had

at the time it's not bad.

But later it hurts

and there you lay.

Maybe for years

you avoid the tears.

But one day stops

there is hell to pay.

Taking the stuff

can never be enough

but cause your death.

Pleasure fades away.

After All

Pleasure is fleeting.

Pain is a feeling

of deep loss

that will not go away.

Remember friends

follow all trends.

Experience the pain

after all play.

Take the pills.

Do what wills.

Stay high and die.

Pain crumbles clay.

Be fresh and don't delay.

Moderate all that may

come to catch you.

Live a good life and pray.

Daryl Eigen

24: Stand Up

Darkness unfolds deeper than death.

Wings flapping midnight holds.

Screech of night searing light

lapping shores and smoldering heath.

In a word is a world.

First love then emotion.

Up and down all around

some day still quiet and calm.

A storm brews; the lake shimmers.

Roads are fluid. The heart simmers.

Bubbling up never stops.

The brim cupped a finger touches.

Worn edges, blossoms bloom.

A lingering crisis darkens the room.

Colors heard. All's absurd

but shining will.

Stand up.

25: Panic Attack

My breathing getting faster,

shortly in full pant.

I am dying, surely I can't be.

Bile rising.

Choking my throat with acid.

A swallow finding its way

between breath and vile;

mouth breathing the while

the best it could.

Nose filling with tears.

From belly came all fears,

threatening to scream. I

sat up in bed, feet to the floor.

Walking the planks ever more.

For a minute did panic abate.

If only I could breathe.

I could almost hear the siren

of the ambulance I did not call.

Daryl Eigen

If death it would be too late;

if panic it would soon be over.

Slowing my breath without avail.

Urged to run with nowhere to bail.

Trapped again in my bunker.

Awaiting the rocket

to land squarely in my hole.

A flare popped overhead

lighting the barren landscape

casting shadows below.

They were coming.

Cans were clanging on the wire

The mess hall was on fire.

If only I could breathe.

26: Ocean of Tears

He remembers

feelings of grief

in late September

a moment too brief.

Fall winds blowing

the desert nights cold.

He missed his calling

to stew in anger untold.

On the surface he looked OK

not looking down the rails.

Little things gave him away

tiny tears rolled down the trails.

Winter came as crisp air

nothing like the jungle steam.

His breath frosty and lips bare

in limbo between a snarl and a scream.

Darkness came early

Daryl Eigen

As did the thundering hoofs of defeat.

He used to be surly

but now was in full retreat.

He checked the perimeter.

He checked the lines of fire.

He checked regrets,

but never forgave her.

He checked and checked, never to tire.

Another night to wrestle shadows.

Another night not to cry.

Another night to have no windows.

Another night to get by.

To himself he kept

his mind still at war.

He was in sadness but never wept.

Homeless he lay, thoughts afar.

27: Time Passing

As a time traveler

I sit in my big winged chair,

watching the world

change faster and faster.

I hardly remember how I got here.

 It wasn't pretty.

Life is the stuff sausage links are made of,

best kept in the back kitchen.

The calendar spews dates

like a popcorn machine.

Watching the sun arc across the sky.

A fine summer's day where

balmy breezes worry swirling grasses.

Under the old oak, children of the woods

try to surround its girth.

The day is filled with pretend and exploration.

 A whistle blows and Mother calls us home.

Daryl Eigen

The war happened and never un-happened.

Face each day.

Sit down to breakfast.

By the time I start

it is dinner-time

nothing has been done.

Not even a cup of coffee made.

Night falls, stars spin circles of long

exposures whilst the earth turns.

Mother died.

Life accelerates

one moment to the next

Youth spent like a freshly broken egg

between fingers irretrievably

separating tomorrow

from yesterday.

Next day was 50 years hence.

Did I spend it the right way?

After All

I can count my regrets

but not my inattention.

After All

28: Feel Normal

There are good days and bad days...

This is a bad day.

Retired early... had to.

Too tired to work

Too tired to run.

Too tired to drive.

Unable to lead, never to succeed.

In pain he could slowly walk.

The sidewalk stretched ahead

 like a grey undulating ribbon.

An obstacle more than a way

morphing too quickly into a bridge.

With will he walked the span

After All

high enough to make him cringe.

Imagine the crunch if he fell.

The sirens, bells and farewells.

Darkness enveloped his thoughts.

He did not jump or cry out loud.

Or even ask why the black cloud.

He just wanted to feel normal.

And walk effortlessly with the crowd.

29: Down, Down, Down (1,4,9)

One day a threshold is breached.

And the tremor begins.

Other symptoms become apparent.

And the world s l o w s d o w n.

Symptoms are odd and pervasive.

Side-affects and symptoms are confused.

Try to swallow without choking.

Don't trip and fall to the ground.

Is your mind slipping? Is it the war?

Is it your age? Or is it the all?

Did you abuse too much?

Or forget too much?

Or is it your ancestors

from the line o n d o w n

Down, down, down I go.

Where will it take me?

After All

Who is to blame?

Is it the royals? Is it the crown?

Did it happen in the war?

Was it AGENT ORANGE after all?

Made by an evil corporation

Our Government let us down,

Covered us with a secret poison.

Without even a second look

or a serious frown,

The stage was set for killing

all that is living

Were we clowns for not realizing

that we were already dying?

Were we faithful for no reason,

bringing death around?

Were we lost and hoping to be found?

But left for dead

in the silence of no sound.

We defended a small mound

with casualties by the thousands.

Daryl Eigen

We were hungry and dirty across the pond.

We died with nobility early and

of duplicitousness later.

We were tired then and we are still

down, down, down.

30: Limits

4 minutes to breathe,

4 days to drink,

4 weeks to eat,

80 years to live, give or take

with good health.

Check gas or charge,

batteries die,

smoke alarms beep,

all night long.

Moonlight looms large for a time.

Sleep happens,

temporarily,

intermittently,

un-expectantly.

Hear the alarm.

Stay awake --- for awhile

Daryl Eigen

Spiritual Poems

31: In Between My Thoughts (8)

There was a moment

between my thoughts

when I realized

I had thoughts.

And I realized

I was

not those thoughts.

There was a moment

between my thoughts

when I realized

my thoughts revolved

around and around

going the same way

again and again

digging a deeper

Daryl Eigen

trench of tendencies

with each revolution.

There was a moment

between my thoughts

when silence did ring

ringing ripples of color

reverberating through

the such-ness of life.

There was a moment

between my thoughts

when the darkness spread

like comfort and honey

gobbling up everything

I did right and I did wrong.

There was a moment

between my thoughts

when the deep well

After All

of grief and terror

welled up and smothered

my world in a

torrent of tears

flooding myself

tearing my heart

drowning my life

choking my breath.

There was a moment

between my thoughts

when the lightness of light

shined from every angle

of being

lighting the darkness

replacing the darkness

filling the rips

in the fabric of

my existence.

Daryl Eigen

There was a moment

between my thoughts

when the fire burned

in my eyes

burning my plans

burning my ambitions

burning my being

Burning my memories

past and future

sacrificed

mere cinders now

There was a moment

between my thoughts

when I was nowhere

but here

and nothing

but that

there was a moment

without thought or movement. Just a moment

32: Time Analysis

Three aspects all:

before, during, and after,

in the still moment.

in the midst of laughter.

in the ringing silence.

Anticipate and meditate

Enjoy and participate.

Remember

the lily on the water,

the flashing of the leaves.

Forget the future;

let go the past.

Where are you?

Stay close not low.

Cast a noon shadow.

Daryl Eigen

Future is imagined

before is ever more.

Now is real.

Past is past ever after

but has some appeal.

Choose today

now is here.

Ignore the bloody tear

locked in amber

for a future year.

Number your days

For time is choice.

What's right, what's left?

Clouds weeping.

Flowers wilting.

Time hurries downhill

After All

healing wounds for friend and foe.

Older still a blessing also.

Strings of pearls of chosen worlds.

Fast and slow, little time, moments lost.

Clock's numbers and dials

for time has one direction.

Look inward to shining spirit

all is brilliant when present

nothing less than vivid is-ness.

When time stops, it stops for you.

Mums bloom like fireworks

softly muffled against a lit sky.

Is there an after? If so why?

33: I Saw Him (1,3,5)

I saw him today.

Kind of a buddy

filled with tubes.

Nothing to say.

I saw him today.

Was I family?

No, just a friendly,

surprised they said OK.

I saw him today.

Know him not well

except he was swell.

Closed eyes he lay.

Antiseptic smell

anyone could tell.

Softly toll the bell,

After All

wide eyed at death's knell

Small rooms and halls

pulsating breathing walls.

Rushing in my ears

near deep in tears.

He usually said hello.

Asking if I

were high or low,

a good guy.

He was Army.

I was Marine Corps.

It didn't matter,

he needed an encore

Machines of death

surrounded him.

Whirring loudly

Daryl Eigen

testing his health.

Sedated,

partially naked,

partially breathing,

partially living.

Every room held a vet.

Every room had an angel.

Every room filled and set.

Waiting for spirit to be met.

I said a prayer.

Many thanks for their care.

Silent and none too fair

I was made aware.

A sob and a gasp

from another room.

Still lost my grasp

After All

hurrying from gloom

Professionals I passed,

ghosts in the night.

Alarms gave fright

monitors glowed with light.

Nothing could I do.

Never he knew.

I quickly bid ado,

my turn not yet due.

I saw him today.

34: By and By (1,2,4)

By and by I think I am dying again.

The waves of death

are lapping at my feet.

Waiting to drown me.

Sitting in a room looking out a window.

It is crystal clear but death

is a cloudy foe.

The sash shimmers

the pane glimmers.

By and by I think I am dying again.

The waves of death

are lapping at my feet.

Waiting to see me.

At a party talking to a friend.

The conversation takes an ugly trend.

After All

The mouths are gabbing,

tongues are jabbing.

By and by I think I am dying again.

The waves of death

are lapping at my feet.

Waiting to swallow me.

I am sitting talking to you.

I lose my hands, feet and eyes too.

My body is going; my self is exploding.

By and by I think I am dying again.

The waves of death

are lapping at my feet.

Waiting to consume me.

Not if, not when, but how?

Just fading away is digestible.

My mind fears other possibilities.

Daryl Eigen

35: Pixelated Recycling

Out of the corner of my eye

I have the vision, no ... the idea

of what I see.

I am afraid to turn my head and look.

I feel it is my demise fast approaching.

I once had a dream where God

was tearing up the old rug

of experience in a golden haze of fine pixel

dust swirling in shafts of light.

Black Unicorns and dark hooded hobbits in

attendance, shadows dancing on the walls.

Rainbows good and bad

 chewed up by the digital Kali,

 the last recycler of nature.

Maybe to start again.

Am I to be pixelated,

After All

recycled by the dark helpers?

They are in the dust looking for me.

This is not a dream nor is it real.

Hopefully, just a peripheral disturbance.

But anyway I am afraid.

36: Dark Matter

I sit here like last year

traveling near the speed of light

I can go no faster

try as I might

I fly around the gravity bowls

entering into swirling galaxies

each powered by a black hole,

whose dark face is deep cold.

I feel its invitation to fall

forever slowly into its grip

sitting on the event horizon

I hear the sound of Om

A roaring like a water fall

now past the point of no return.

Ignore the sound of the call

thinking there is no more to learn.

After All

Time and space become distorted.

Observers grow old and die.

It was reported I never aged.

Now there is no one to be counted.

My mind expands through my eyes

I see Krishna's face beyond space

frightening even the wise

as it is a place of no lies

My ship is made of carbon

where have I gone?

I cannot remember

anything of what's been.

I broke the sound barrier eons ago.

I mock the mach I used to travel

maximum speed I go.

Why I can't go faster, I may never know.

Daryl Eigen

It is a mystery, an enigma

I came home too late

shortly after I left.

No worries, all is past.

  Black holes are matter,

  but matter not.

  Unlit celestial bodies

  hardly account for the missing.

  What is dark matter?

  Strange particles made of knot.

  Black cats without a smile?

Not a black hole grey with guile.

Still eating its neighbors,

the black hole glows and shakes.

In the dark night,

in the darkness of light,

I hope I lived a life of right

37: Too Many Lives

I have some questions:

Will I have to pay for my sins?

If so, will the debt be paid

in the same currency it was incurred?

Does the last judgment mean no more judgment?

What if you were the greatest offender?

Or does it mean the final terrifying

judgment of me and my misdeeds?

I am sorry...... No really, I am sorry.

Do I have to come back.

to another life to pay this debt?

Can I get a chapter seven in heaven?

Can I be saved?

Who will pay for my sins?

Will my son or daughter be asked

 to pay in this lifetime?

Daryl Eigen

Not in my lifetime not in any time.

How many lifetimes will it take

to pay for my crimes and misdeeds?

Is there a Tibetan Buddhist Hell realm

I need to avoid?

I am too human to come back as a cur.

I pray it is so.

Or is my real Self a movie screen?

 Remaining pristine no matter

 the films of our lives?

I hope it is so.

I learned some prayers

 to help me when I die.

But I sometimes wake

 in sheer overwhelming terror:

 I am dying.

I walk around until it becomes

so intense that I wake my wife.

On the way to the ER I recover.

I forgot to say my prayers

38: Writers Guild

All the dark places

edit 'til right.

lay open to light.

Vulnerable crazies

fighting to write.

Therapy some say

for others OK.

No matter we write

Sometimes sleep

sometimes trust,

words we keep,

write we must.

High desert poems

novels and essays.

Old open wounds,

new neural pathways.

Daryl Eigen

Tears leak

cries in the dark

images too stark

once a week.

Writing from a distance

building high castles.

Missing all who work

in rhymes, missives, and epistles.

39: Brick Wall

I hit a wall, a brick wall.

It was the end of a long haul.

I tried it all

But no further could I go.

I made a call

But nobody answered.

 In despair I took a fall.

Even so I struggled to stand tall.

With no one to help

I gave it my all.

Daryl Eigen

40: That's All

After all is said and done

I just want to go to bed.

Enough has been said

to annoy the dead.

After All

PRIOR PUBLICATION AND AWARDS FOR ESSAYS AND POEMS

1. VA Hospital, Albuquerque, New Mexico
2. Heartbeat, January 2014
3. Heartbeat, July, 2014
4. Veterans Voices, Fall 2014
5. Veterans Voices, Spring 2015
6. Veterans Voices, Summer 2015
7. VA 2014 Arts Contest, Regional 1st Place
8. VA 2015 Arts Contest, Regional 1st Place
9. DAVA State of Kansas 2014 Award
10. In Memory of Our Women by WAC Veterans Association OVESA CULP Hobby Chapter 61, Dallas, 2014 Editor's Choice Award,

The parenthetical numbers at the end of the titles denote the prior publication and awards of the poems or essays as listed above. (10/1/20150)

ABOUT THE AUTHOR

Daryl Eigen, served as a combat Marine in Vietnam in1966 and 1967 and was awarded 3 Purple Hearts and the Combat Action Ribbon. He is the author of "A Hellish Place of Angels", a war memoir (www.ahellishplaceofangels.com) , as well as numerous scholarly articles in several disciplines (www.daryleigen.weebly.com) Daryl received a MS and BA from the University of Wisconsin-Milw., a second Masters from the Institute of Transpersonal Psychology, and a Ph.D. in Engineering from Northwestern. Daryl was a Bell Labs MTS where he created popular telephone services like Calling Card service and the AT&T audible logo. He was a contributor to the digital optical network and held a number of senior management positions including CEO for several high-tech start-up companies. Daryl is the proud dad of Tony, Lori, Molly, and Sarah and grandfather to Amelia, Sophia, Zoe and Norah. Daryl currently writes on a variety of topics and lives in Portland, Oregon with his lovely wife Jeevani.

Proof

47693762R00065

Made in the USA
Charleston, SC
13 October 2015